Bluer Than This

Acknowledgments are due to the editors of the following magazines and journals in which some of these poems first appeared: *Ambit*; *Arca* (Romania); *Blue Cage*; *Fatchance*; *The Frogmore Papers*; *The North*; *Pequod* (U.S.); *Poetry London Newsletter*; *The Rialto*; *Romania Literara*; *Scratch*; *Seam*; *Slow Dancer*; *The Squaw Review*, 1993 (U.S.).

'Perfect Health' appeared in *First Draft*, edited by John Bosley, Stephanie Bowgett, John Duffy & Philip Foster (Albert Poets, 1994).

'Failed Sonnet Home' appeared in *What Poets Eat*, edited by Judi Benson (Foolscap Press, 1995).

'Apples' appeared in *The Long Pale Corridor: Contemporary Poems of Bereavement*, edited by Judi Benson & Agneta Falk (Bloodaxe, 1996).

'Seven Year Ache', 'You Did It! You Did It!' and 'Self-Portait' appeared in *Poems For The Beekeeper*, edited by Robert Gent (Five Leaves Publications, 1996).

'Safeway' appeared in *Eating Your Cake... And Having It*, edited by Ann Gray (Fatchance Press, 1997).

'Chet Baker' and 'Charlie Parker in Green Shoes' were published in a somewhat different form in *Ghosts Of a Chance* (Smith/ Doorstop Books, 1992).

Bluer Than This

John Harvey

Smith/Doorstop Books

Published 1998 by
Smith/Doorstop Books
The Poetry Business
The Studio
Byram Arcade
Westgate
Huddersfield HD1 1ND

ISBN 1 869961 87 0

British Library Cataloguing-in-Publication Data. A catalogue record for this book is available from the British Library.

Designed and typeset at The Poetry Business
Printed by Garian Press, Huddersfield

Distributed by Littlehampton Book Services Ltd, 10-14 Eldon Way, Lineside Estate, Littlehampton BN17 7HE, tel 01903 828800

The Poetry Business gratefully acknowledges the help of Kirklees Metropolitan Council, Yorkshire & Humberside Arts and the Arts Council of England.

Cover picture: 'After Corot' 1979–82 *by Howard Hodgkin, courtesy of Anthony d'Offay Gallery, London*

CONTENTS

7   What Would You Say?
8   You Did It! You Did It!
9   Talking About Cities
10   Chet Baker
11   Driven By Rain
12   Slow
14   Indian Lake
16   Out of Silence: Squaw Valley, 1995
17   Lilac
19   Self Portrait
21   Interior With Roses
23   Failed Sonnet Home
24   The U.S. Botanical Gardens, Washington D.C.
25   Sometimes I'm Happy
27   North Coast
28   The Wrong Wind
29   Couples
29   1 Edward Hopper: 'Room in New York', 1932
30   2 Edward Hopper: 'Excursion into Philosophy', 1959
31   Perfect Health
32   Upper Street
33   Moonwalk
34   Passing On
36   Apples
37   Charlie Parker in Green Shoes
39   The Americans
39   1 Ranch Market, Hollywood
41   2 Nanny. Charleston, South Carolina
42   3 Crosses on the site of a road accident. U.S. 91. Idaho
43   Safeway
44   Playing At House
45   Always Chinatown
47   Seven Year Ache
48   Blue Settee
49   After Corot
50   Spellbound
52   Valentine
53   By The Numbers
57   Blue Monk

What Would You Say?

What would you say of a man who can play
three instruments at once - saxophone,
manzello and stritch - but who can neither
tie his shoelace nor button his fly?

Who stumbles through basements,
fumbles open lacquered boxes, a child's set of drawers,
strews their contents across bare boards -
seeds, vestments, rabbit paws?

Whose favourite words are - vertiginous,
gourd, dilate? Whose fantasy is snow?
Who can trace in the dirt the articular process
of the spine, the pulmonary action of the heart?

Would you say he was blind?

Would you say he was missing you?

You Did It! You Did It!

'It was Roland Kirk, wasn't it?
Who played all those instruments?
I saw him. St. Pancras Town Hall.
Nineteen sixty four.'

The same year, in the old Marquee,
not long out of college, cocksure,
I saw Henry 'Red' Allen,
face swollen like sad fruit,
sing *I've Got the World on a String*
in a high almost falsetto moan,
proclaiming the truth beneath
the song's exuberant tone –
and married you – desperate to dull the ache
I thought simply came from being alone.
Eight years of slow denial later,
both at the end of our respective rope,
we broke, raw and gaping, back into the world,
intent on reinventing our lives,
greedy for life as Rahassan Roland Kirk,
on stage in this cold country,
nineteen sixty four,
cramming his mouth with saxophones,
harmonica, reed trumpet, piccolo and clarinet,
exultant, black and blind,
the whoop and siren call of flutes and whistles,
spiralling music unconfined.

> 'You did it! You did it!
> You did it! You did it!'

Daring us to turn our backs,
stop our hearts and ears,
deny the blood wherever it leads us: fail.

Talking About Cities

Horses, she told him, if I'm late
there are these marvellous photos of horses.

What he looks at, crouched low,
face close against the glass,
are still lives: mottled eggs and feathers,
pebbles, nests of grass.

During the war he used to sit
cross-legged with wonder and wait
for the first chicks to wobble and wave
their stubby wings and run across
his outstretched hands.

When he tells her this
she dismisses it for what it is:
another sly metaphor for fatherhood.
It's the horses she loves,
their wild beauty, uncontained,
the way their necks strain hard against the frame.

Outside, though, walking on the embankment
in the sun, so many sets of twins
they're difficult to ignore,
and when the clarinetist – really, this is true –
begins *I Thought About You*
she springs sideways to straddle the wall,
her face against the lazy blue,
and he dares to place his fingers
one by one and warm, safe
inside the nest of her hands,
and this is every city
they have ever seen or will ever see.

Chet Baker

looks out from his hotel room
across the Amstel to the girl
cycling by the canal who lifts
her hand and waves and when
she smiles he is back in times
when every Hollywood producer
wanted to turn his life
into that bitter-sweet story
where he falls badly, but only
in love with Pier Angeli,
Carol Lynley, Natalie Wood;
that day he strolled into the studio,
fall of fifty-two, and played
those perfect lines across
the chords of *My Funny Valentine* –
and now when he looks up from
his window and her passing smile
into the blue of a perfect sky
he knows this is one of those
rare days when he can truly fly.

Driven By Rain

After reading Tess Gallagher's 'Amplitude'

And when finally I look up, lost,
from this book, I'm shocked
by the sudden wash of rain
that blows in swathes along this slow
suburban street I'm trying to call home.
So strange, the way it can be there from nowhere,
filling out your world, everything you see: memory.

That day we climbed almost to the summit of Cadillac,
so hot you went skinny-dipping in the lake
while I sat propped against hard rock,
drank from our thermos and read,
only stopping when you emerged, glistening and ready,
eager to make the most of our time, the weather ...
And then, when we clambered, exhausted,
over the last broad grey stones,
the sky, from nowhere, black with thunder,
those first stabs of lightning fixing the peaks
opposite and closer by the second, so that,
yards only short of the summit, we turned
and ran, laughing with panic, leaping over rocks,
newly wet and slippery with rain, never losing our footing,
me clinging to your hand as if my life depended upon it,
which of course it did.

Slow

> *for Lee Harwood*
> *and in memory of Paul Evans, 1945–1991*

It was all right until the slow lurch towards
Battersea – the Power Station in decay – that new
building you always pointed out as we went past ...

A small stone loosed into the valley like memory, so far
you cannot hear it fall.   All day I've kept this at bay.

Walking with Lee along the front by the sea, ruins
of the old West Pier, shift and change of housefronts
between Brighton and Hove.
Small cups of coffee, thick and black; we go out
for focaccia and cheese and bring them back.
Photos of Paul Evans in Lee's room, child in his arms.
Two years I sat in Paul's classes as soft-spoken
he opened poetry before me

                'Here ... read/
                        listen to this ...'

                He was dead instantly, it said.

So trivial
            anything I fear or feel compared to this

The way when we crossed the river your heart leaped

                'Remember walking back to our cabin in Maine in the
                in the valley ... None of this is gone from my memory
                although thinking about it makes me weep.'

At the station Lee and I shake hands, spurred on
by talk and art, poetry and poets, Dada and the Surreal,
the kids who live with him alternately through the week.

I board my train so far from death and you: alone
in the compartment read memories of Paul – friends,
daughters, wives. Signals shuttle us from side to side.

        The river.

For one more moment I am here with you

        ('you move me – and the thought of you')

The walk I will never take, child in my arms,
slow, to where you have set up your cameras down by the bay.

Indian Lake

And you are reading
and I am reading
and beneath everything
the soft rush
of your breathing,
the slow fall of page
on slow page,
the sudden crack
and flutter of the stove,
the sun that has burned down
to a nub of orange haze,
its last breath lifting
off the water,
leaving an empty
plane of white
where colour once has been;
and in reflection
the massed hump
of the far bank
pitches effortlessly forward
into the lake without
breaking for an instant
its perfect surface.

Over on our neighbour's
half-cleared lot,
a boy of high-school age,
interested, his father says,
in nothing but sports
and girls – he drives
his four-wheel up the dirt
road, up and back,
churning up the torpor
of the afternoons –

shuffles his feet across
the dust, adjusts
the slow bounce
from hand to hand
before the sudden
upthrust glance,
the curl of ball towards
the unguarded metal hoop.

Here in the cabin
you have set down
your book, uncorked
the wine, your own
glass close beside the
pan, the hiss of fat
as you slice in thick
rounds of sausage,
tomato, onion rings,
accepting this old
division of labour
knowing tomorrow
will be different,
so much will change,
remain the same.
For now it's enough
to savour the smell
of sausage frying, turn
another page. Dark
through the window,
the last vestiges of Indian Lake
visible between the trees.

Out of Silence: Squaw Valley, 1995

How the light diffuses round house corners;
Redwood walls, the breaking colour of packed earth,
Ochre in the mouth;
The red woodpecker testily chiselling sap from a small ash
The only sound in the valley;

Helpless in the face of all the times I failed you.

Lilac

5 or 6 and drying me from the bath
warm before the fire, my father said,
a glance across his shoulder, we'll have
to stop this soon, in front of your mother,
you're getting to be a big boy now.

And so I entered those years of ignorance
and shame, doors quickly closed and clothes
pulled down, the Sunday paper cancelled,
the book of drawings my uncle had
exchanged for his leg in France
no longer in the wardrobe drawer,
those packets wrapped in newspaper
and stuffed into the dustbin rusted through
with blood – all disappeared from sight.

Though I remember once, playing table tennis
with my mother, mesmerised as she bent low
to scoop the ball across the net,
the way her breasts swung loose beneath
the thin brown cotton of her top
and me flushed there, struggling to ignore
even as I strained to see, I suppose
I was 10 or 12 by then and old enough
to wonder what a breast might be.

I did not think of this for years, mother,
for there were girls, I found, less careful
with their bodies, women too, until that
Christmas, my father dead and scattered
to the ground, when you released yourself
from hospital so we might spend together
that last festive time and I carried you
from bed to chair and chair to bed,
lifted you onto the toilet and pulled up
your dress, eased down your pants,

bones unfussed by flesh
that crumbled a little more each time,
like chalk against my hands.
We did this unspeaking, unashamed,
the slow washing of pain
as I ran the flannel across your ribs,
the shadows of breasts that hung
like bruised lilac against your chest.

Self Portrait

Bonnard at Le Cannet

Cold here, this room you sit in, 1945;
your corner table, vase of flowers and white cloth,
grey scarf close about your neck,
you sit and smoke, patient for cognac
warm in its glass; a white cup with gold rim,
the small black coffee she will bring.

Again and again sketched in his diary,
Saturday, February 26th, Tuesday the 15th of June,
like an otter, she would ease, sleek, into the bath,
snug against the curve of porcelain.

On the radio, news of the Armistice,
a hastily articulated peace, the Jews.
The air is rimed with smoke, far echo of guns.
The small electric heater stands unplugged,
no fire in the grate. Marthe – why does she not come?

Those last mornings you have walked
between the almond and the olive trees,
gazed over red roofs toward the fullness of the sea.
You painted ochres, oranges and browns,
cupboards steeped in jars and bottles,
herbs in bunches, greengages and plums,
golden apples, persimmons.

In the studio the slow shunt of trucks,
smell of paint thick on your hands;
stiff-legged before the mirror,
you blow warmth into your fingers.
Head shaved, ready, this is not so difficult,
one portrait, all that's left.

A gash of colour for the mouth,
those veins, blue, drawn down
across the fabric of the face,
black hollows where the eyes would have been,
burnt out by bodies that lay ripening,
close-pressed between trees, their richness
leaking back into the soil, out of reach of seeing,
stripped beneath the surface of the sea.

Interior With Roses

Morning. When I fetch the paper a little after six
the pavements are ridged with ice.
In a downstairs room across the street
a man sits under an orange light;
he is writing a troublesome letter,
explaining why his wife and he are separating.
Why is she leaving him? How best to express this?
He reaches out and turns down the lamp.

We went by train to Sheffield to see the Vuillard;
the gallery seemed impossible to find.
Except for one room, the paintings were cramped
and badly hung, the only ones which might
have lifted our hearts we had already seen.
Patches of red askew at the edges of beds,
a shirt thrown carelessly across a leather chair,
his mother sweeping out the room, moss roses
straining for the sun. A few more days
and they'll be strewn across the dark wood floor,
the door open so she can hear him cross
to the window where he switches on the lamp,
the scratch of nib on paper as he writes.
The orange hue that runs through everything.

The house where we first lived together,
geraniums in boxes at the windows,
the orange patio where we'd sit with fruit
bought from the Chinese brothers in the market –
oranges, peaches, plums – juice bright on our mouths and hands;
the table where sometimes I sat and wrote.
The man across the street has finished or just given up,
his wife has called him to the table, mushroom-barley soup;
a dash of red beneath the orange cloth,
the room spotless, swept,
the roses on the dresser already leaning;

in a day or two, maybe tomorrow,
their petals will begin to fall.

The broom stands in the corner and the shirt
has been folded neatly in the drawer.
When I walked home to where you waited,
winter roses framed by London brick,
fresh smell of coffee, music streaming out –
all I had to do, step to the open window,
call your name, walk in.

Failed Sonnet Home

The windowboxes outside the Clocktower Café
are delirious with bloom. Cappuccino with
chocolate and cinnamon. Blueberry muffin.
How many more days can the sky sustain
this absurdity of blue? I can taste vanilla
from the pines. And you. You know the other day
Jake drove me to Truckee in his van
and in Safeway I was stalled mid-aisle
by the scent of that hot-buttered toast
we shared before you drove me to the train.
How far we are away! Crimson columbine,
black centre of violet pansy, its yellow eye –
one thing you learn here: how little soil
it takes to nourish the most stubborn root.

The U.S. Botanical Gardens
Washington D.C.

The floor is azure blue tile
slick with the residue of that morning's watering,
green hose slack between the leaves.
We used to come here, safe, and sit
not touching, humidity high in the nineties
and helicopters hovering, a block beyond the Hill.
Even though you're back in London now
I can trace your sweat, the way, like glass,
it beads round the curve of your raised thigh.
In the display of medicinal herbs, I break
small leaves into my hand:
yarrow, for internal bleeding; foxglove
for the muscles of the heart.

When we meet, a year or more from now, by chance –
the departure lounge at Heathrow; hurrying
along the platform at Gare du Nord;
that harbourfront café, the concert hall –
and when your eyes widen and, uncertain
whether or not to kiss me,
you hold out, instead, your hand,
I will slip into it those remedies I have long carried:
the knowledge that, nurtured, passion flowers
in the darkest place.

Sometimes I'm Happy

A Lester Young Story

Lazy-eyed, light-skinned, hair brushed back from the oval of his face, he gazes from the stand: couples discreet over their third or fourth martini, loud from the rear booth, laughter, a shot and a beer; the pianist in the pick-up band, no better and no worse than last night's or the night's before. With a hitch of his shoulder, Prez brings his mouthpiece to his lips: one more chorus and he can call it a day.

In Bismark, North Dakota, he made his move; quit playing in his father's band and struck out on his own. At 139th Street in Harlem, the bandleader's wife shut him in the closet with recordings of the man he'd been called in to replace, made him listen to that raw-edged, muscular sound. Heavy-chested, a woman with marcelled hair and her mother's hips, she watched his pale fingers as they fretted over keys, his mouth as he slicked spittle on a reed. On stage, when he rose stooped for his solo, the others laughed into their hands or rolled their eyes and missed the filigree of his invention, intricate as a spider's web and strong.

On the road he wrote his mother without fail, swallowed barbiturates, smoked dope, drank gin. The women he met at bus stations and stage doors were country girls: fey, freckle-faced and thin; skinny breasts and bones beneath their huddled coats barely held in place by skin. One or two thought they loved him, heard his voice inside their own, made hope still-born a child between them, syphilis it's twin.

With Basie in the forties, on his feet after the trombone's rasp and roar, paving his way on stepping stones of single notes before striking for home with thirty-two bars of pride and beauty making the moment, the melody his own. The draft officer is waiting for him at the bar. Private 39729502, he served his time in the stockade; desertion, disobeying orders he did not understand.

When finally they discharged him as unfit, unfit was what he was.

He drank more gin to steal himself against whatever pain was rupturing inside; played dinner lounges, one-roomed bars and supper clubs from Oklahoma to D.C. Touring Europe with Jazz at the Phil, sharp-eared young men with suits and glasses followed him around, wrote serious articles re-evaluating his career. His voice on radio, is lighter almost than the air which carries it to our ears. He is tired, wants to lie down, quit. But no – 'You great, man! Fine!'

Up there at the Panther Rhythm Lounge, he shakes inside his loose grey suit. One more chorus, then he can call it a day. *Sometimes I'm happy, sometimes I'm blue, my disposition depends on you.* Blood that seeps, slow and bitter, from his rectum and his tongue.

North Coast

Once, we stayed here, out of season,
arcades and the Magpie Café closed,
clouds massed like bulkheads in the northern sky
and around the municipal grandstand
only the melismatic cry of gulls.
Close by our feet, winter lay coiled like rope.
At night hope hung across the water like a child.
What is never shared, cannot be lost.

When she was seven or eight,
I brought my daughter here to stay,
Our first time in an old-fashioned B & B,
hot water bottles and flasks of coffee on request.
She laid out her clothes, folded and neat,
each item in its proper drawer,
alarm clock wound and set for seven,
books and diary on the square oak table
nudged against the bed.

There have been other lovers, other nights.
The town, I heard this morning, is falling
rock by rock and day by day into the sea.
Tied up against each forecast,
fishing boats, all colours, rack and slide.
My daughter rang me yesterday from France,
she and the man she's lived with for years
are breaking up. I shall come here again, yes,
I think so, with someone else or on my own.
We cling to what we can, and the rest,
one way or another, clings to us.

The Wrong Wind

The wrong wind
marshals its forces along the channel
and that range of hills we can quite clearly see
against the northern horizon
will within moments be lost to sight.

Down in the town
a woman bustles across the bridge
with lowered head, plastic shopping bags
bumping and barging against her legs.

Outside the Jolly Sailors
two dogs pause in their robust examination
of each other's genitalia to sniff the air,
and along the street at number 54, the children's
crossing guard, once assistant harbour master,
taps his barometer and scowls;
the parrot in its cage is one hundred and five
or one hundred and ten, depending
what you believe.

High on the West Cliff
we squat in the lea of blackened gravestones
and count our blessings: peppermints, lip salve,
four squares of dark chocolate, the return
halves of two supersaver tickets
to Pudsey via Leeds and a compass
neither of us can read. A ladybird,
startled, stops its scuttling run along your arm
and braces its wings for flight. Too late now,
too foolish to make a dash across
open ground, we wait, and if our luck holds
the worst of the storm will pass us by.

Couples

1. Edward Hopper: 'Room in New York', 1932

With one finger she picks out the tune
the way her mother showed her,
slow afternoons when the dogs lay aside
their indifferent barking and moths
hung sleeping from the inside of the blinds;
distant rattle of ice inside her mother's glass
and whatever burned inside her
cold water and calamine could not touch.
In the close air of their apartment she has been
thinking more and more of those times.
The newspaper rustles behind her, whatever
her husband is reading commands his attention.
Although he has loosened neither
waistcoat nor tie, the yellow distemper
of the walls has begun to sweat.
The red dress she is wearing
has a bow bunched high at its back,
like a flower that once, petal by petal,
he would have reached out and unfastened
before her mirrored eyes.
His shirt so white that to turn and look
at it would be to be blinded by the moon.

2. Edward Hopper: 'Excursion into Philosophy', 1959

He has been reading the *Tractatus*, Wittgenstein,
the footnotes make him laugh; the book open
on the bed, the blue divan. How to explain
the duality of grief and joy, relief
and guilt. The way her breathing, as she lies
behind him, legs drawn up, exposed,
her back not quite touching his, touches his heart.
They've been together fifteen years
and he would like to leave it at that.
The sun burns low along ripening wheat
that looks like the wheat in the painting by Van Gogh;
the postcard she bought him that day in Portland, Maine,
and told him if he ever left her she would truly die.
He picks up his book and begins to read,
but sets it back, drawn to the window by the sun,
the sound of a meadow lark in the field.
The only signs in the morning they were there
will be her red hair, snagged at the corner
of the pillow; the slight impression, fading,
on the mattress where they lay.

Perfect Health

She was a dancer then, Tucson: shared one floor of her house with a gay choreographer who when things were especially bad would climb silently into her bed at three and curl into a ball against her back – a memory of her cat.

She said she had danced in Paris and it was true. A basement club near Pigalle, a company of six; her solo routine involved a giant pack of cards, a roulette wheel, a croupier's green shade – nothing left to chance. They would meet after the show at three or four, the girls from the Moulin, the Paradis, the Crazy, sit and smoke and pick at food and bitch – that café in Montmartre with the fish, the all-night pizza place on the corner of the Champs Elysées. But Tucson was where it happened.

She met him by accident, she always said, her husband, and that's what it turned out to be. Not that it was easy to tell – such natural elegance she could walk away from a five-car wreck still looking like an angel touched by grace. 'Didn't you used to be a model?' folk would say. 'An actress?' 'A dancer?' She smiles and shakes her head and continues on her way.

If he had broken every bone in her foot he would have been kind.

The last time her mother wrote it was to say she'd cleared out all those silver cups and medals, carriers of dust. 'If I had a daughter...' she begins, but knows better than to let that thought run on too far. These things she clings to like a barre: when she sits, her neck and back form the same precise line as when she was seventeen; with no-one else watching, in the centre of her room, she can perform an almost great plié – when all is said, her knees aside, she still has perfect health.

Upper Street

Now the rain is falling
and the petals that have already fallen,
pink and white, float up around us as we walk,
your smile suggesting how close you are to forgetting
the lover who so recently left you,
and so we continue, ducking into a corner pub
and there, facing you, I catch myself doubting
if I will ever feel more closely drawn to you
and I can tell we are both wondering
about this dwindling distance between us,
how perilously a kiss would close that space.

Back outside the rain has eased
and we cross the street in search of the restaurant
a friend of a friend has recommended,
but when we arrive the sous-chef is new,
the manager took over only two weeks ago,
the waiter who sleeps alternate Tuesdays and Thursdays
with the friend of your friend has taken the night off
and our eyes glaze over the menu,
and, neglecting month or season,
settle for grilled oysters, half a dozen each.
Rejecting the house red, we land by chance
a Côte du Rhone, so peppery we can ignore
the confusion around us and relax, slack-shouldered,
like figures in a Vuillard painting.
When they arrive the oysters are delicious!
Drizzled with a sauce of butter, garlic and white wine,
dashed at the last second with lemon,
they're set sizzling before us, surfaces
sharp and golden, soft and alive on our tongues,
bright in our mouths and eyes.

Moonwalk

Full moon from Bejing to Washington Square.
A VCR spills its numbers out across
the room, and on the deck a solitary jay
lands with not quite control. Nights
when all he can do is trace the blue pulse
faint along the vein, those fickle haemoraghings
of need like blips on a screen, notions of her
that nudge against the bone.

The way the plane, just at the moment of
descent, jolts his eyes up towards that broken ring
of peaks, their crescent of snow; the moon
that filtered slow through cloud that evening
on Prince Street, late, after Raoul's, more than a little drunk,
and not unhappy when she asked him home.

The kiss she places on his mouth is just a kiss,
the trajectory she follows is not the one he thinks:
so close it's no longer a matter of distance or direction,
only gravity – the need to place one foot
after another, find balance, move on.

Passing On

It sounds like the beginning of a story and of course it is. He walked into the room where she was standing by the piano singing *Alice Blue Gown* and fell in thrall – in love, too, though these are not the same – this lean-boned woman in a slender dress, velvet, the only good dress she owned – and it seems incredible to me, but he must, this man who could not stammer in public without blushing, he must have walked up to her, this woman whose sophistication he had known only from movies with Bette Davis or Joan Fontaine, and asked her name.

Helen.

And my father, a foot soldier in any Grecian army, handsome it was true, lacking what she would see as nobility and grace – what did she see in their place, whose father had left her, oh, so many times? I think she saw humility there, fidelity, the sense that once she had blessed him with her smile he would never leave her side.

Look at them here, this photograph, the breakwater at Ostend, the first year of their marriage, six months before the Phony War: his swim suit, the strap over one shoulder, the kind Johnny Weismuller wore; the way she leans towards him, claiming him, the breasts in her striped suit that disappeared, it seemed, before they were mine to hold or suck. My father, I imagine, likewise; those ten years my narrow bed was stationed at the foot of theirs and I witnessed through veiled eyes as they presented chaste backs to one another and undressed. Soon after we were rehoused and they withdrew into the dignity of single beds.

Later still, she became ill. Lived a wheelchair for nine years. Used her frailty to blackmail me home. Learned with an illusionist's timing the exact moment of my father's heavy settling to call for what she wanted from some other room. Adult to adult, she outfaced my cursing, words my father never would have said, in love or anger – closed herself upon my pleading – 'For Christ's sake, can't you see what you're doing?' Drove him, sick and broken-hipped, emphysema corrupting his lungs, six months, a year, early to his death.

These and other things I cannot forgive. Failing, not as my father did, married more than thirty years whatever else. I love him for the love he gave to her who even in memory I can hardly love.

I want to hold my father, tell him, look, I'm okay; kiss his face.

Apples

My father is dying.
Scent of apples from the night stand.
I reach out my hand and rest
one hard against my face;
he taught me how to tell the real thing
from the fake; hold it close beside the ear
and shake – a genuine Cox, the seeds
will rattle loose inside their case.
You see. He told me
and I swallowed every word by rote.
Five cotton towns of Lancashire,
five woollen towns, four rivers
that flow into the Wash – Witham,
Welland, Nen and Great Ouse.
Once learned, never forgotten.

My father is dying.
He died nine years ago this June.
They phoned from the hospital
with the news. His face a cask
once used for storing living things.
A cup of tea, grown cold and orange
on the stand beside the bed.
Length of his fingers, nails like horn,
unclipped. Though dead,
my father is still dying,
oh, slowly, sure and slow as the long fall of rain.
I reach out again for the apple
and bite into its flesh
and hold him – bright and sharp,
safe inside the hollow of my mouth.

Charlie Parker in Green Shoes

Back in the City, I walk south on Seventh,
cut across Broadway, joust with the traffic
round Times Square; finally hit 42nd Street
around 6th Avenue. From the squeak
of the subway doors as the train sways
the tracks crosstown, to the buskers
in Bryant Park, hustling out-of-towners
on their way back from brunch,
music pumps beneath your feet.
Ornithology, *Dizzy Atmosphere*, *Constellation*,
Groovin' High – Bird, who died at thirty-five,
each year called to do the work of two,
but still that's not enough.
'Bird Lives!' tagged on the walls,
the scrape of chalk and spray of paint
seguing into his last breath.

No heaven's hip enough to hold him!

Out on remission, he scores from a dude
on roller skates in Washington Square,
picks up a fifth of Seagrams and hits
the Magic Shoe Store where he buys –
wait for it! – green shoes.

He remembers his first record date,
thirty dollars, union scale; Dean Benedetti
following him everywhere, pockets overflowing
with wire spools, magnetic tape, keyhole saw,
the slender lead and microphone
lowered over the stand, recording every note
Bird ever played. He remembers the first night
at the club Chan Richardson walked in –
high heels, high colour, black hair.
Tastes Chinese dinners, barbecued ribs,

sandwiches custom-built – three layers
of smoked fish, Chicago corned beef,
green tomatoes, kosher pickles, coleslaw.
A snack. Smack. Scuffling bills from friends
and strangers in the men's room and out
along the street. He feels the wind
that whipped his head as he roamed the city,
rode the subway, Battery Park to Harlem,
Brooklyn into Queens; he sold his horn
a hundred times, his heart but not his soul.
Cirrhosis of the liver, stomach ulcers, pneumonia –
he would do it all again.

Horn out of hock he heads for 52nd Street
but the west end of the block is all but bare –
Jimmy Ryans, the Onyx, Downbeat, the Samoa,
Spotlite, The Three Deuces, The Famous Door –
all back to the dingy brownstones that stood before the War.

The only gig he can get is depping
with the Junkyard Angels at the Lone Star Café.
Midway through *Close Up the Honky Tonks*
he's had enough, rips open his sack of salt peanuts
and blows them all away.

Next morning, early, two repo men
with neat pony tails, sift careful
through the ashes.

'Green shoes?' they say, perplexed.
'Green shoes?'

The Americans

1. Ranch Market, Hollywood

Who would have thought she'd get this far?

Not her teachers,
riding her forever about the way she spoke,
slow, out of one side of her mouth;
the slovenly way she sat in class,
skirt hiked past her knees;
assignments neglected, forgotten, rarely done –
that obstinate wedge of gum.

Not the boys who paid admission
to the drive-in, Coke floats and root beer,
her gaze never shifting from the screen
as hands pressed and pressed her breasts,
legs locked tight like ice.

When she laid the entry form
for Miss Junior Dairy open on the kitchen table,
her mother laughed right in her face.

But she knew all about Lana Turner,
spotted in Schwab's Drugstore on Sunset;
that Arlene Dahl – the most ravishing
redhead of the silver screen – had been
the Rheingold Beer Girl of '46,
and this new one, Novak – wasn't that
her name? – discovered touring
as Miss Deepfreeze after working
in a five-and-ten cent store.

Finally she stole ten dollars
from her mother's boy friend's wallet
while he slept; caught a bus as far west
as she could and hitched the rest.

Here at the Ranch Market
the hours are long, tips are poor,
but at least you get to laugh.
One of the other girls goes Tuesdays
to an acting class and she thinks
one of these nights she'll tag along.

For now, she's happy
so close to the heart of things.
Just last week George Brent walked in
off the sidewalk and sat right down –
regular coffee, black, one jumbo hot dog,
18 cents, and the chilli, 5 cents extra.
Sometimes, when she'd seen him in the movies,
she'd wondered if that neat little 'tache
was stuck on, maybe, but no, close up,
she knew it was for real.

2. Nanny. Charleston, South Carolina

They don't want me to hold this child. All them righteous brothers with the anger and their shades. Sisters, too. Wave placards in my face and shout and spit and sound their horns. One of them come right up to me, standing here with this precious boy in my arms, and says, 'Sister, can't you see that's the Devil's child?' Well, I ain't his sister, nor about to be, ain't got no sister 'cept Merilee, and she passed on having her third. No, if there's anything I am, it's this child's mother, near as can be, doing everything for him his own mother don't do. 'Sides, you just have to look in this sweet baby's face to know he ain't no Devil. See that sweet little angel mouth, way that skin shine so white and flawless like a doll's; and his eyes, how they stare out at you, never looking away, not blinking, like they already owned the world.

3. Crosses on the site of a road accident.
  U.S. 91. Idaho

It started when I told Jerry not to take the wheel. Look at you, I said; he was so close to falling-down drunk, if it hadn't been for the way he was bouncing off the walls, he'd have been eyeballing the floor. Will you get a look at the state you're in? Well, of course, it was the last thing I should have said. I mean, whatever else he was, sober or drunk, that Jerry always was the world's most cussed son of a bitch. Besides, by then we'd already hit on these two girls, dark-skinned, like maybe they had some blood in them, you know what I'm saying, and the way they was swallowing down shot after shot, barely stopping to wipe their mouths across with the backs of their hands ... Hot! Jerry grins at me when we're out to take a piss. Hot and not a day past fifteen. He was wrong about that. The taller one, Marcie, she was sixteen years, three months, so it turned out; Sheryl, she would have been seventeen three weeks this Labor Day. Anyway, Marcie and me climbed right in the back, Sheryl up front with Jerry, real close, one of her legs hooked across his knee. We had this pack of Coors swimming in a bucket of day-old ice down by my feet. Petey, Jerry said, swinging round his head, pop me one of those. I saw his face, just for that moment, bright in the headlights, Jerry having the time of his life, smiling his cock-eyed smile.

When they rolled the truck back over and reached inside, mine were the only arms that reached back.

Safeway

I like a woman who knows her way to Safeway
but will pack me off there anyway,
a list fixed to the refrigerator door –
'wonderful lettuce,' 'big dill,' 'great
tomatoes,' 'serious bread.'
Who will be there when I get home,
closed inside her dark room, safe light glowing red.
And I will tiptoe to the kitchen,
juggling misshapen bags and packages,
wallet, checked-off list and keys;
set each and every thing quietly in the place
bestowed for it – as quietly as lollo rosso
wrapped in cellophane will agree to go.
But a woman who will slide her hands
across my eyes the instant I step through
the door and have me turn toward her face,
the soft grey vest across her breasts,
sweet and supple sweetness of her skin.
And after we have risen from the wreck
of fallen groceries, either she or I will slide
a garlic-basted chicken from its bag,
uncork a bottle of that Merlot
and take them both to bed,
sitting in the soon-to-be sweaty whiteness of sheets,
breaking the chicken with our hands,
aware of the joy of this and each other's
eyes, the juice that runs along our fingers
and gathers in the deft spaces inside
our arms and behind our knees, waiting
to be found there later, savoured, licked away.

Playing At House

Just a few days and my eyes seek you out,
automatically, where you sit, bringing meat
and cheese to your mouth without tasting,
each slice so thin it breaks against your hand.
And setting out later for the house coincidentally
we share, returning home, I fall in step beside you,
your dancer's step so like my daughter's,
flex of calf and taut of thigh; though we were walking
under the merest sleeve of moon I could see
the exact blue of your eye.

Light shining still, I step into your room to say
goodnight and instead of retreating then
behind my door across the hall what I want
is to sit all night in your room, not touching,
or ride, warm beside you, in the rear seat of a car
funnelling through the gloss of dark, radio playing,
hairs of our arms soft and coarse as those that wait
alert inside the lavender of a mariposa lily;
patient, breath caught on the air, our bodies held
in balance: never arriving, always travelling.

Always Chinatown

Not another of those urban myths exactly, not the way he told it, the Texan country-folk singer at the Union Chapel, how this friend with both wife and mistress, finally called the mistress from his wife's home and said into her answerphone, clearly, after the tone: 'This is the sound of a breaking heart,' then shot himself once, pistol pressed against his chest.

These last few days the trees have catapulted into leaf and flower, dyspepsia of bloom. While you take your bath, I walk out to buy coffee and bread for the breakfast we will share, eyes shielded from this new intensity of light. The joy of doing normal things: reading papers, Saturday afternoon movies, frisbee in the park – I didn't realise you had never seen Chinatown before.

Nor other things …

We are sitting in what had always been our favourite restaurant. Early evening and all around us theatre-goers, lovers, foreign tourists with this page of their guide book folded down. At your back, a mother and her grown-up daughter, purchases slewed around their feet, are enjoying the day's special, drinking wine. 'You know I never trusted him,' one says, lowering her head, and despite myself I'm drawn into their story, the boy friend's casual infidelities, the stepdaughter's shenanigans, the sure lure of this narrative, its anticipation and fall, all distracting me from the moment you set down your fork, push the fringe of hair clear from your face, your voice slowly building now, the baroque intricacies of another tale, its subtle twists and turns, dead-ends, disguises, strangely familiar lies and alibis – I recognise it now, too late, not yet the ending which I neither second-guess nor understand …

And then I do. That most clichéd of them all …

Outside on the street you ask me for a final hug and I suppose, somehow between the scaffolding, your arms, and the laughing passers-by, it happens, because suddenly I'm walking away, blind, between city traffic, no sense of where to go or what to do, no way to know if you are standing still at the side of the road as taxis thread, black, behind your back, or whether you have already turned and with a pale shoot of hand, flagged one down. Nevertheless, small and clear, I hear the click of your tongue, quick against the roof of your mouth, as you raise your face to say another name, a new address, anticipation like salt on the rim of your lips.

'Forget it, Jake. It's Chinatown.'

Seven Year Ache

'There's nothing so spiritual about being happy
but you can't miss a day of it, because it doesn't last.'
Frank O'Hara, 'Poem' *('And tomorrow morning at 8 o'clock')*

A memory, then? Bright in your red braces
you jump late from a cab outside the coffee house
where I sit dumb among brioche and coffee beans –
Colombia Medelin Excelso, Organic Papua New Guinea –
silenced by your smile.

Listening to the radio this afternoon,
thumbing through my well-worn life
of Frank O'Hara, its pink and purple annotations,
I notice *Top Hat* is on TV in time
to see Fred and Ginger shelter in that convenient bandstand
and marvel at the grudging way she mimics his routine.
And I think of the young O'Hara
watching them for the first time from those
red velvet seats of the Worcester Warner's.
How he loved them! Ginger's 'pageboy bob',
Fred's 'peach melba voice'. Watching them now,
I hate Astaire's dinner-suited smugness,
the certainty he'll get the girl at the end.

Last night, and then again today, I'm taunted
by the bizarre easiness of dying; O'Hara at forty
knocked over by an errant jeep on the beach; his mother,
frail from hospital and drying-out,
tumbling yellow roses into his grave. Such waste!
Each day that's lived is lived in hope and in regret.
We die each day and not from love but lack of it:
the pull of your hand away from mine, the turn
of your face aside. Whatever flowers you throw
on that fresh-turned earth will carry with them, bright
and unremarkable, the stench of what was missed.

Blue Settee

After reading Tess Gallagher's Portable Kisses

This kiss is made of remembering,
of not quite remembering enough;
the movement of her mouth
that rarely seems to mesh with his –
strangely, he likes this. This kiss deep in her pocket,
torn cinema tickets and small change; the way
they use their tongues.
This kiss starts high at the nape of the neck
and makes a new map of the world;
it moves them from the clumsy darkness
of the hall, into failing sunlight
where they practise compass movements on the bed,
their way lit by candles and Chardonnay, his tongue
crossing hers mid-ocean as she turns
beneath him and floats free, their breath
sounding an itinerary of Irish Sea, Atlantic Ocean,
and on down the coast of Maine.
Timetables. Taxis. A blue settee. The sweep
and blur of skin. She could tell him anything.

After Corot

'After Corot' 1979–1982, by Howard Hodgkin

the train turning into the bay
enough to bring tears to your eyes

sleeping, your skin ivory
reach & fall of your breathing

                your hand

in the painting everything is
at a distance: cliff, harbour,
sea, sky

tight within a frame
    within a frame

only wait
and the light breaks white
on the horizon, mastheads etch
contours green beyond the wall's bulk
and as a small boat painted red hoves into view
the land slips another foot into the sea

you throw up your arm

untrammelled,
blue seeps under the edges of the frame
refusing to be bound

the rocking of the train
as it rounds the slow curve

your waking breath

the sea

Spellbound

Out for our walk early,
long before the mist has been burned
off by the sun, fast along
the path past Jack Straw's Castle
and the Whitestone Pond,
till, entering the tree-lined terrace
of the old Pergola – first slim shoots
of new growth thrusting upwards to its roof –
we light on the curve of lawn
to see first one foolhardy rabbit, then another,
cropping at the grass, so heedless, they must
have read the sign, NO DOGS ALLOWED
and left the rest to trust.

In the park café, children run amok
according to the current fashion; patients
huddle with their carers and the smartly dressed man,
recently retired, each hair in place, sits
with his ritual tea and toast, while you and I,
in the splendour of this early spring,
sprawl outside on metal chairs, relaxed
among sections of that morning's paper,
half-a-dozen items of as-yet-unopened post,
and, determining with all true and proper seriousness
what it is we should do with our lives,
almost before the words have left our mouths,
decide in our hearts to take a different course.

Resolute as on that day six months before,
I met you off the morning train, your face
so pale and strained I thought you must be ill,
till, leaning across me in the cafeteria
of that gallery, you told me that to see
one another any more, to continue with this –

you would not call it relationship – affair,
was out of the question; the pair of us running,
an hour later, hand in sweating hand, your
appointment cancelled, resolve in shreds,
up onto Waterloo Bridge to hail a cab and race
back to the place we now call home and bed.

Valentine

Is this the way it will be?

We scrunch up against winter glass
watching for a break in the cloud
a breath of sun

This fall of water   This stand of trees
Sweet Chestnut   English Oak

On the far pond the heron
unveils grey wings for flight

      Last spring we sat in pale sunshine
      on an outcrop of rock
                  oblivious
      as the tide marooned us

Nine months on
we cradle china mugs   read books   draw stars

Inside you
new life turns with each swelling of the tide.

By The Numbers

After 'Inventory' by William Corbett
from his Columbus Square Journal: 1974–75

Five letters so far today,
three postcards, including
one from my friend Al in Mexico,
hopefully writing sestinas
somewhere south of Guadalajara;
a many-times resealed brown envelope
brimming with poems badly typed
yet charged with spiritual content
and the energy of God's good grace
and mine to publish should I only
say the word. One apple, one banana,
several handfuls of mixed dried fruits,
four coffees, each one stronger than the last.
My first whisky, Talisker or Highland Park,
I save for later and Art Pepper's keening saxophone –
Leicester it was I saw him, eighty-one or -two,
that false summer that flared so bright before he died,
and now I sit listening to him play
Too Close For Comfort, waiting for you,
not counting the minutes till I hear
your key against the lock, refusing to;
the table laid, sweet potato and fennel soup

already simmering on the stove,
five cheeses ready on the plate –
Vignotte, Blue Stilton, Cornish Cheddar,
a stump of somewhat sweaty Feta,
Raclette – the first raspberries of the season,
bought this morning at the market
in Berwick Street, you carried them home
and hurried out again, leaving me the task
of printing out the two hundred or so
addresses from our updated list of friends –

seven Romanians, two Bulgarians,
the odd Norwegian, that young poet
I aim to publish from the Republic
of Moldova; two Danes, the woman
Geoff was forever trying to get off with,
the one from Macedonia.
That done, I sit out on the balcony,
catching the late evening sun –
purple geraniums brought back
from the garden centre, dahlias,
lobelia, petunias, richly purple
and dark-veined, a pair of white
impatiens to break up the colour –
my father, were he living, would
have opted for some simple daisies,
marigolds, the climbing roses
he cut and trimmed so carefully
before setting on my mother's table.
How many close relatives left
among these labels? One son,
one daughter, several cousins,
much removed. All day I have been
dipping in and out of books, James
Schuyler's Diaries, Sapphire's *Push* –
Ben Sidran's *Talking Jazz*. A week
ago we moved however many
hundredweight from shelf to floor
and back again – fourteen Jim
Harrisons, ten Thom McGuane,
the complete Lawrence in that white
Penguin edition, each with its small
photograph, coloured and bright;
Ray Carver and Tess Gallagher, close
if not quite side by side; Hammett,
Chandler, Elmore Leonard,
James M. Cain. There was a time
I would count and catalogue everything:
movies, poems, plays; girls I was in love

with, girls that I might one day marry,
girls I would go out with if I could;
notebooks that went with me from
the Rex, East Finchley to the Everyman,
the Curzon Mayfair to the Gate,
the Electric Cinema on Portobello
– now closed – to the Academy
in Oxford Street, long gone.
A proliferation of Bergman and Fellini,
Hawks and Ford, whispered words
and stolen kisses – an education,
as Frank O'Hara said, of quite another kind.
The balcony of that cinema, recently reopened,
in Camden Town, the sweat and bluster,
embarrassment and sighs. Oh, Carol
with no E, where are you now?
Fifteen, you seemed a decade older,
saw the world, clear and dangerous
with quite another eye.
Who would have thought then
we would know as little as we
know now? How many friends
are living, how many have died?
My good friend, Tom, from whom
I learned so much, not least
the power of righteous indignation;
Tom, after whom my wife and I
named our son, would be the same
age as me now had he lived.
Mitchum, slow-eyed and heavy
shouldered, with his ballet dancer's walk,
has died, I see, at only sixty nine;
James Stewart, one day later,
still haunted, I'll wager, by the
frightened beauty of Kim Novak's eyes,
finally succumbed at eighty-one.
I cling with not-so-quiet desperation
to the years of those who soldier on,

active beyond their time:
Harry Gold, still blowing bass sax
with his Pieces of Eight, played his first
gig in nineteen twenty three;
Benny Carter soloing elegantly
on alto in New York at eighty nine.
The list, thank God, goes on.
The other night I watched Compay
Segundo, suddenly after ninety years
in Cuba, a world recording star,
playing his patent seven-string guitar,
his leathered face lit up by laughter
and the hope that danced on in his eyes.
There is this to do and that to do,
a dozen tasks already for tomorrow,
others forming in my head,
one last espresso, Veluto Nero,
as we sit here, legs and bodies
touching, stretched along this fond
settee, talking about today, tomorrow,
all the days that come after –
infinite and uncountable.

Blue Monk

For all the world as if he has just walked in off the street, a gas company official, a removal man, something humdrum; when he sits at the piano it is as any man, unconcerned, might sit at a bench in the park, ease the weight from his feet, so palpable, the relief with which he sinks, broad, into the quilted leather of the seat; his topcoat, which he makes no attempt to undo, strains tight across his back, one or two stitches at the shoulder have snapped; squat on his head Monk is wearing a black and white checkered hat.

And now a scattering of applause has started haphazardly around the hall; it is an age before he edges back his cuffs and stretches out his hands.

*

Driving through Camberwell
the rain slides black across the windscreen
and as we pass the lights for the third time
you push a cassette into place,
the click and hiss of tape and then it's him.
Rhythm-a-ning. Charlie Rouse on tenor, Sam Jones on bass,
Art Taylor at the drums. New York City, February, 1959.
A hundred years ago.

* *

The critics at this time damn him with scant regard, another black jazzman touring Europe, parading his few tricks for a handful of krona and a pocketful of praise. But tonight, in Rotterdam or Oslo, Gothenburg – where doesn't matter – this is different. Monk is on. Audience forgotten, that oversize right foot pounds down at an awkward angle; this is not the night to watch a legend running through what legends do, respectfully, and so the crowd cranes forward, reaching for the fire that flares so unexpectedly, so close to the end of this life.

Inside his overcoat, under his chequered hat, Monk is lost and doesn't care if he's never found. Doesn't give a good Goddamn. His fingers stab at single notes, crush chords; roll with the tide then tighten down. His hands seek and find warm spaces lost between the keys, laughter strung across the dark like lights of fishermen spaced out along the beach, phosphorescence on the sea, like Whistler's *Nocturne in Blue and Gold*, the glow of radio stations long into the night.

* * *

I carry my wine across the room to where you sit
and we stare out across this London square, these London streets.
I hear draw up outside the cab to take me home.
What if, on that precipice of kitchen, all those years ago,
instead of rinsing those last dishes at the sink,
I'd taken both your hands in mine and said
I would go with you, no matter where, no matter what?

* * * *

Monk gets up from the piano as casually as he sat down, troubled by the memory of a promise he once made and now can neither remember nor forget. In the small hotel room with a view over the air ducts and the kitchens, a bottle of brandy stands half-drunk beside the bed.

I can never again watch your dress
fall to the floor or rest my breast
against your breast, my mouth pressed
to yours to stop it with a kiss.

C minor, F 7th, B flat –
nothing can be bluer than this.

NOTES

'What Would You Say?'
'You Did It! You Did It!'
After I'd read the first of these poems at the Aldeburgh Poetry Festival, someone came up to me from the audience and, in response to its riddle, said the lines about Roland Kirk, the jazz multi-instrumentalist, which now begin the second poem. It was a gift I couldn't refuse.

'Chet Baker'
'Charlie Parker in Green Shoes'
The first poem, occasioned by trumpeter Baker's death on falling from the window of an Amsterdam hotel in 1988, has changed only marginally since its appearance in the earlier collection, *Ghosts of a Chance* (1992). The second piece, however, has taken on a whole new central section, largely as a result of reading and later recording it with the jazz group, Second Nature.

The results of that recording – which includes all four poems mentioned above, plus others – are available on cassette, and soon on CD, from Slow Dancer Press, 59 Parliament Hill, London NW3 2TB.

'Couples'
Edward Hopper's paintings, highly suggestive of urban narratives as they are, were the starting point for these poems as they have been for many others. *Edward Hopper and The American Imagination* (Whitney Museum of American Art/W.W. Norton, 1995) includes prose and poetry inspired by Hopper's work by Paul Auster, Tess Gallagher, Thom Gunn, Walter Mosley and others. Rebecca Goss has a fine take on 'Room in New York' and another Hopper painting, 'Hotel Window', in her pamphlet *Keeping Houston Time* (Slow Dancer, 1997).

'The Americans'
Robert Frank's book of photographs, taken on the road in the 1950s, are the basis for this sequence of pieces. Originally published by Robert Delpire, Paris in 1958 and by Grove Press, New York in 1959, with an introductory essay by Jack Kerouac, they have recently been republished, along with Kerouac's essay, by Scalo Publishers in association with the National Gallery of Art in Washington D.C.

'Always Chinatown'
Jake Gittes, the detective hero played by Jack Nicholson in Roman Polanski's terrific 1974 film of Robert Townes' screenplay, concludes his investigations – and the movie – a little more aware and far more powerless than he started out.

'Seven Year Ache'
The idea for this came from reading *City Poet: The Life and Times of Frank O'Hara* by Brad Gooch (Knopf, 1993), and the title is borrowed from a wonderful 1981 album by the singer Rosanne Cash. Thanks, Rosanne!

'After Corot'
A few postcards aside, my first encounter with Howard Hodgkin's paintings was in the Anthony d'Offay Gallery in London in 1993 and what struck me most then was the intensity of the colour. Walking round a major retrospective at the Metropolitan Museum of Art in New York two years later, I began to realise the extent to which so much of Hodgkin's work is balanced between the abstract and the representational. Overwhelmingly, though, his concerns seem to be with light and colour and the shifting relationships between them.

More recently and closer to home, a large show at the Hayward Gallery in London gave me the chance to look at a range of Hodgkin's paintings again and again. By the time the show was over, I had two favourites – both small, each by way of homage to other, earlier painters: *After Degas* and *After Corot*. I can still remember exactly where they hung on the walls.

And this is my small homage to Howard Hodgkin; a way of saying thanks. I'm pleased and proud to have a reproduction of his work on the cover of this book.

I am greatly indebted to the students, staff and organising body of the Squaw Valley Community of Writers Poetry Week, where, in 1993 and again in 1995, many of these poems were first written and discussed. My especial thanks go to Rachel Conrad, Sands Hall, Brenda Hillman, Robert Hass and Sharon Olds. My thanks are also due to a number of other writers who have commented on and contributed to these poems in various ways, in particular Alan Brooks, David Kresh, Rhona McAdam, Nancy Nielsen and Ruth Valentine.

John Harvey is a writer, publisher and occasional broadcaster. His sequence of Charlie Resnick crime novels has earned widespread critical acclaim and has been translated into more than a dozen languages.

He is also an adaptor, for radio and television, both of his own work and that of many other writers including A. S. Byatt and Graham Greene.

He lived in Nottingham for many years, but has returned to north London, where he continues to run Slow Dancer Press.

Bluer Than This is his second collection of poetry.